S0-AXN-313

Swashbuckling SCOUNDRELS
PIRATES IN FACT AND FICTION

ARIE KAPLAN

TWENTY-FIRST CENTURY BOOKS / MINNEAPOLIS

For Aviya Leah Kaplan, the best daughter on the seven seas!

Twenty-First Century Books
A division of Lerner Publishing Group, Inc.
241 First Avenue North
Minneapolis, MN 55401 USA

Main body text set in Columbus MT Std 12/15.
Typeface provided by Monotype Typography.

For reading levels and more information, look up this title at www.lernerbooks.com.

Library of Congress Cataloging-in-Publication Data

Kaplan, Arie.
    Swashbuckling Scoundrels: Pirates in Fact and Fiction / by Arie Kaplan.
    pages cm
Includes bibliographical references and index.
    ISBN 978-1-4677-5252-7 (lib. bdg. : alk. paper)
    ISBN 978-1-4677-5253-4 (eBook)
    1. Pirates—Juvenile literature. I. Title.
G535.K17 2016
910.4'5—dc23   2014026704

Manufactured in the United States of America
1 – VP – 7/15/15

CONTENTS

Johnny Depp's exciting exploits in the *Pirates of the Caribbean* films are based in part on the adventures of real-life pirates.

Swashbuckling pirate captain Jack Sparrow and his blacksmith friend Will Turner take to the high seas to save a kidnapped beauty, retrieve a stolen ship, and lift a long-held curse. Along the way, they clash swords with villainous Hector Barbossa, British naval officers, and other deadly foes. As many filmgoers will recognize, this is the plot of *Pirates of the Caribbean: The Curse of the Black Pearl*. The 2003 film launched the wildly popular *Pirates of the Caribbean* movie franchise, which over ten years raked in more than $3 billion at the box office. But while piracy is the stuff of popular movies and novels, it is also the work of real-life criminals, running through history from ancient times to the twenty-first century.

A DISAPPEARING ACT

Often the stories of historical pirates are just as colorful as those told in modern-day pirate movies. One of those real-life tales comes from April Fools' Day 1696. On that day, a small, plain-looking sloop (a ship with a big mainsail and small sail in front) arrived at the harbor at Nassau, capital of the Bahamas, a group of islands in the Caribbean Sea.

smaller boat. The landing party made a beeline for the home of Nicholas Trott, governor of the British settlement on the Bahamas. A crewman named Henry Adams, who spoke for the landing party, told Trott that the ship sitting outside Nassau's harbor was the *Fancy,* a private warship with a crew of more than one hundred men. Adams handed Trott a letter from his captain, Henry Bridgeman. In the letter, Bridgeman claimed that the *Fancy* had recently been in Africa transporting slaves and had grown desperately low on provisions, with a crew that was in dire need of shore leave. Bridgeman requested permission to sail the *Fancy* into Nassau's harbor with no questions asked. In exchange, Bridgeman would give Trott the *Fancy* itself, as well as gold and silver coins valued at 860 British pounds. British governors then typically made a salary of 300 pounds a year, so the offer was tempting.

Before giving Bridgeman an answer, Trott quickly called a meeting of the colony's governing council. He neglected to mention the money and the ship that he'd been offered. Instead, he told the council that the *Fancy*'s presence was quite imposing and might deter enemy French forces from attacking Nassau. He also pointed out that the *Fancy*'s crew would be able to help defend the city if needed. The council agreed to let Bridgeman welcome the *Fancy.*

Shortly afterward, the sloop entered Nassau's harbor, and the rest of the crew came ashore. They unloaded a cargo of huge amounts of gold, silver, and jewels. Bridgeman also came ashore and gave the governor silver and gold coins, as well as the *Fancy.* When Trott boarded the sloop, he saw that he'd also been left a generous tip: 50 tons (45 metric tons) of elephant tusks, one hundred barrels of gunpowder, chests brimming with muskets and other guns, and a huge collection of ship anchors. It was clear to Trott that Bridgeman was trying to buy his silence with these gifts.

Trott also saw musket balls lodged in the *Fancy*'s deck and sails damaged by cannonballs. He suspected that the glittering treasures brought ashore were not from dealings in the slave trade. They were spoils attained through other means—illegal means. Trott believed that the *Fancy* was a pirate ship and that Bridgeman was a pirate captain. Trott had a choice. He could alert the British authorities to Bridgeman's whereabouts or turn a blind eye and pocket the loot. He chose to take the treasure.

What Trott didn't know was that Bridgeman was in reality Henry Avery, one of the most successful pirates of his generation. Dozens of British ships were combing harbors and seaports around the world, looking for Avery and his crew. Was Avery in Calcutta or Bombay in India? Was he in western Africa or in Madagascar off the eastern coast of Africa? In fact, he was in Nassau, drinking at a local pub after having bought off Trott.

In 1695 British pirate Henry Avery captured the *Ganj-i Sawa'i*, an Indian ship carrying gold, silver, and other treasures. This engraving from the 1700s shows Avery in the foreground. Behind him, his pirate ship attacks the *Ganj-i Sawa'i*.

After landing in Nassau, Avery retired from life as a pirate. His crew went their separate ways. Eventually, six of them were caught, and they were executed in London, England. As for Avery, he was never apprehended. Nobody knows for certain what became of him.

"MARINE HEROES"

Avery was a wanted man, a known criminal. However, not everyone took a negative view of Avery and his fellow pirates. A book called *A General History of the Pyrates*, published in 1724, about three decades after Avery disappeared, refers to pirates as "Marine Heroes, the Scourge of Tyrants and Avarice [greed], and the brave Asserters of Liberty." In

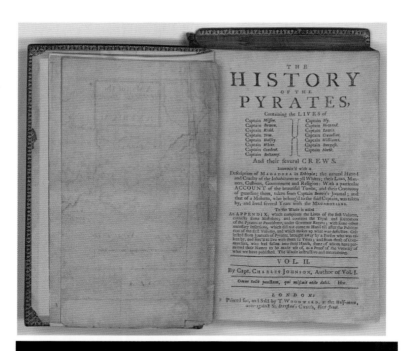

People have long been fascinated by pirates. In his 1724 book, British writer Daniel Defoe chronicled real-life pirates of the Caribbean.

this case, the writer (believed to be British novelist and journalist Daniel Defoe, writing under a pseudonym, or false name) was being sarcastic. But some Europeans of his era did look upon pirates as heroes. By then pirates had acquired a reputation as rugged individualists, keen on carving out a life of freedom and self-reliance, away from the tyranny and conformity that clamped down on many European societies.

The myth of pirates as noble, heroic, lovable, even comic figures is still strong in modern times. In reality, however, pirates are dangerous and sometimes bloodthirsty criminals. In legal terms, piracy is an act of criminal violence, theft, or robbery committed on the ocean or on a smaller body of water. In different eras and in different parts of the world, pirates have been known by other names, including freebooters, corsairs, buccaneers, and brigands. Pirates have been around for centuries and have operated worldwide.

Starting in ancient times, merchant, or cargo, ships traveled across seas and oceans, carrying valuable goods to trade in far-off lands. Such ships were targets for pirates, who would steal the cargo to sell for their own profit. In the course of raiding ships, they would sometimes murder crews and passengers.

Many historical pirates were born into poor families and resorted to piracy as an escape from poverty and for the promise of money, freedom, and adventure. In the twenty-first century, pirates still sail some of the world's major sea trade routes. Like pirates of earlier eras, they too turn to piracy to escape lives of poverty and desperation.

Whether in fact or fiction, pirates are rugged outlaws. But are they murderous scoundrels or lovable antiheroes? Or does the truth lie somewhere in between?

Pirates have been around since the waterways of the world were first used for commerce. The earliest known historical documents to mention pirates describe a group known as the Sea Peoples, who terrorized the Mediterranean Sea around 1200 BCE. Ancient texts say that these pirates invaded eastern Anatolia (in what became modern-day Turkey), Syria, Egypt, and other lands bordering the Mediterranean.

THE PIRATE AND THE EMPEROR

Less than one thousand years later, in the 300s BCE, a fearless pirate known as Diomedes challenged Alexander the Great, one of the ancient world's most powerful leaders. Alexander's vast empire included the eastern Mediterranean Sea, where pirates attacked merchant ships loaded with cargo.

One legend says that when Diomedes was brought before Alexander to face punishment, everyone expected Alexander to sentence Diomedes to death. Instead, the emperor demanded to know what gave Diomedes the right to sail the seas, taking things that were not rightly his.

Diomedes responded defiantly, by asking the emperor what gave him the right to invade territory and take lands that did not belong to him. Diomedes argued that because he used only his own ship to attack vessels, he was considered a pirate. But because Alexander used a mighty army and navy for similar purposes, he was hailed as a great leader. Diomedes concluded by saying that he didn't know which of the two men was the greater criminal but that if he had Alexander's resources, he would be an emperor as well. Alexander was allegedly so impressed by the pirate's boldness that he let Diomedes go.

TARGET ROME

Pirates also preyed on ancient Rome, based in what became modern-day Italy. In the early 60s BCE, a band of pirates from Cilicia (an ancient kingdom in what became modern-day Turkey) began hijacking Cilician cargo ships, especially slow-moving ships filled with grain bound for Rome. In 67 BCE, they set fire to the Roman port of Ostia and looted inland villages. Roman leaders were alarmed and demanded a counterattack.

The Roman Senate directed General Gnaeus Pompeius (known as Pompey) to lead the charge against the pirates. Securing Rome's grain supply—a major source of food for the empire—was Pompey's first priority. He concentrated his naval forces in the western Mediterranean, in areas that provided Rome with much of its grain and other food sources. Pompey's forces surrounded the Cilician pirates and easily captured them in just a few months.

After the Roman Empire fell in the fifth century CE, overseas trade declined on the Mediterranean Sea. Piracy declined there as well.

PILLAGERS FROM THE NORTH

From the late 700s to about 1100, sailors from Scandinavia (modern-day Norway, Denmark, and Sweden) traveled around Europe via rivers and seas. Known in modern times as Vikings, they conquered territory; raided villages; and stole silver, gold, and other valuables from ships.

PIRATE HOME BASES

VIKINGS Scandinavia

British Isles

North Sea

Baltic Sea

ASIA

EUROPE

Black Sea

Caspian Sea

SEA PEOPLES, CILICIAN PIRATES, CORSAIRS, and BARBARY PIRATES

THE WAKŌ

Sea of Japan

Yellow Sea

Mediterranean Sea

China

East China Sea

Japan

AFRICA

Gulf of Aden

India

Arabian Sea

Somalia

South China Sea

RED FLAG FLEET

SOMALI PIRATES

INDIAN OCEAN

SOUTH ATLANTIC OCEAN

Madagascar

AUSTRALIA

ANTARCTICA

NORTH AMERICA

Great Lakes

NORTH
ATLANTIC
OCEAN

PACIFIC
OCEAN

*Gulf of
Mexico*

Caribbean
Islands

GOLDEN
AGE PIRATES,
BUCCANEERS,
and
PRIVATEERS

*Caribbean
Sea*

CENTRAL
AMERICA

SOUTH
AMERICA

SOUTH
ATLANTIC
OCEAN

"HERE OLAF [A VIKING]
BROKE DOWN [THE TOWN
OF] TAMWORTH AND A
GREAT SLAUGHTER FELL
ON EITHER SIDE, AND THE
DANES HAD THE VICTORY
AND LED MUCH WAR-BOOTY
AWAY WITH THEM.
WULFRUN [AN ENGLISH
NOBLEWOMAN] WAS SEIZED
THERE IN THE RAID."

—Anglo-Saxon chronicler, 943 CE

While most Europeans looked upon Vikings as pirates, they were not outcasts from their own society as were many other pirates of the era. Vikings did not spend all their time on the water. For much of the year, they worked at home as peaceful farmers, merchants, and craftspeople. But when they took to the rivers and seas, they were ferocious. They traveled in fleets of swift wooden warships and attacked victims with axes, spears, and swords. They raided towns and farms, carrying off horses, cattle, and crops. They sometimes also took human captives and brought them back to Scandinavia to work as slaves. And Vikings often raided churches and monasteries, stealing religious objects adorned with gold and precious stones. Once they had secured their loot, they set fire to homes and other structures before departing in their ships.

Attacking with heavy iron axes, swords, and daggers such as these, the Vikings terrified their victims and caused widespread death and destruction.

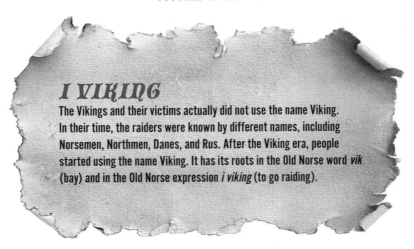

I VIKING

The Vikings and their victims actually did not use the name Viking. In their time, the raiders were known by different names, including Norsemen, Northmen, Danes, and Rus. After the Viking era, people started using the name Viking. It has its roots in the Old Norse word *vik* (bay) and in the Old Norse expression *i viking* (to go raiding).

To save themselves from Viking raids, some groups bought the pirates off with territory. Others signed peace treaties with the Vikings. Other groups fought back. In the 900s, Scandinavians began to adopt the Christian religion, and the Christian Church discouraged many Viking activities, especially the taking of other Christians as slaves. By about 1100, the Vikings had given up their raiding and returned to a more settled life in Scandinavia.

PIRATES FOR HIRE

Piracy resurfaced in the Mediterranean region in the 1200s. By then the Islamic religion had spread from the Arabian Peninsula, across the Middle East and into Turkey and North Africa. Hostilities raged on and off between the Christian nations of Europe and the Islamic Ottoman Empire, based in Turkey. Each side hired privately owned ships, crewed by pirates for hire, to attack enemy vessels on the Mediterranean. These pirates were called corsairs.

Two of the most legendary corsairs were the brothers Aruj and Hayreddin Barbarossa. Part of a family of corsairs from Lesbos, an island off the Turkish coast, the Barbarossa brothers made their fortune attacking European ships in the Mediterranean on behalf of

An unknown painter created this picture of Hayreddin Barbarossa and his corsair crew slaying European enemies on the Mediterranean Sea during the early 1500s. Barbarossa attacked European ships on behalf of the Ottoman Empire.

the Ottoman Empire. By 1512 Aruj, the elder brother, commanded a squadron of twelve ships. In 1516 the brothers successfully drove Spanish forces out of the North African state of Algiers. In 1518, when Aruj died, Hayreddin took charge of operations. He continued working as a corsair until his death in 1546.

THE *WAKŌ* MENACE

Piracy of this era was not limited to Europe and the Middle East. In eastern Asia, from the 1200s to the mid-1500s, bands of pirates known as the wakō menaced the seas around Japan. These pirates included many former Japanese soldiers and fishers.

From 1543 to 1546, Japan was plagued by droughts. Crops wouldn't grow, and many people went hungry. Poor and desperate, many Japanese farmers joined the ranks of the wakō. Later, thousands of Chinese and other Asian pirates joined the wakō, expanding their reach. Some of these pirates snatched grain from Chinese government barges. Others raided Chinese villages, stealing silks and metal goods, which they could sell in Japan for high prices. The Chinese authorities had prohibited overseas trade as a way to cut down on piracy. But this prohibition only made the wakō more successful, since they were able to trade their stolen cargo with no competition from legitimate Chinese merchant ships. According to one commentator, by 1563 the Japanese wakō had 137 vessels crewed by more than fourteen hundred men.

China finally put an end to the wakō in the late 1560s. Its well-trained soldiers attacked the pirates at sea. In addition, China eliminated the ban on overseas trade. As a result, people in other countries could buy Chinese goods from honest merchants, which cut into the illegal smuggling business. Divisions in the ranks of wakō leadership further contributed to the demise of these Asian pirates.

CHAPTER TWO

THE GOLDEN AGE OF PIRACY

Starting in the mid-1400s, European explorers took to the seas, seeking new territories and expanding European empires. Explorers of this Age of Discovery included Christopher Columbus of Genoa (sailing on behalf of Spain), Vasco Núñez de Balboa of Spain, and Ferdinand Magellan of Portugal. Their sailing expeditions took them to the Americas, lands previously unknown to Europeans.

Spain, England, Portugal, France, and other nations were eager to extract gold, silver, and other riches from the New World, as America was then called. Traders and explorers eventually traversed the globe, traveling from the Americas to the Pacific Ocean and on to Asia. As they sailed, pirates followed them, stealing rich cargoes of trade goods from foreign lands. Many pirates used the Caribbean Islands as a base of operations. From there they could intercept cargo ships traveling to and from European colonies in North, Central, and South America.

LEGAL PIRACY

The Age of Discovery was also a time of warfare, as European powers competed with one another for territory around the globe. To increase their naval power—the key to military dominance at the time—many European leaders allowed privately owned vessels to attack the ships of rival nations. Such vessels and their crews were called privateers. They were much like the corsairs of the Mediterranean Sea. Privateers received letters of marque, which were licenses from a government, authorizing the privateers to plunder and raid enemy ships and harbors during wartime. The letters of marque also stated that privateers would give a portion of their plundering profits to the government that sponsored them.

Some privateers became famous during this period. For instance, in the 1500s, England's Francis Drake raided Spanish and Portuguese vessels. He brought their cargo, including gold, silver, and jewels, to England's Queen Elizabeth I. He also commanded an around-the-world sea voyage. (Magellan had made the first.)

Privateers were often respected sea captains. Sir Francis Drake, for instance, was a famous explorer. He also looted enemy cargo ships and shared his booty with England's Queen Elizabeth I. This portrait was painted by Flemish painter Marcus Gheeraerts the Younger (1561–1636).

During peacetime, European governments sometimes allowed pirates to operate freely. Leaders didn't want to antagonize the pirates, since these same crews might be needed as privateers during wartime. Depending on whether or not a nation was at war, the captains and crews of pirate ships and privateering vessels were often the same people. Sometimes governments hired privateers to hunt especially powerful pirates, blurring the lines even further.

A group of pirates called buccaneers operated early in the seventeenth century. Buccaneers were French, British, and Dutch sea adventurers who preyed on Spanish settlements and ships in the Americas. Buccaneers looted, raided, and pillaged in the same way pirates did. Like privateers, they attacked the trading ships of political and commercial rivals of their homelands. They did so legitimately, with letters of marque from the governments they served. But some buccaneers overstepped—or ignored—the rules outlined in their letters of marque. They looted for their own personal gain and didn't share any profits with the government that had sponsored them.

Buccaneering hit its peak during the mid-1600s. According to historians, the rise of buccaneering marked the initial phase of the Golden Age of Piracy, an era when piracy flourished in the Caribbean Sea and beyond. Many pirates whose names we still recognize come from this renowned age.

"MY NAME IS CAPTAIN KIDD"

Born in Scotland, William Kidd worked as a buccaneer before settling in the North American colony of New York. There he married a wealthy widow. When the War of the Grand Alliance, which pitted England and its allies against France, broke out in 1689, Kidd became a full-fledged privateer in the service of the British Empire. In February 1696, Kidd departed from the docks at Deptford in London on orders from the British government to subdue pirates in the Indian Ocean and to raid any French ships he encountered.

Nearly a year into the voyage, when he had reached the coast of eastern Africa, Kidd decided that rather than hunt pirates, it would be more profitable to become a pirate. He successfully raided many merchant vessels, but his crew members didn't like him and challenged his leadership. During a heated argument with gunner William Moore, Kidd struck Moore on the head with an iron-bound bucket, knocking him dead.

In early 1698, Kidd captured the *Quedah Merchant*, an Armenian ship brimming with expensive cargo from India, including silk, calico cloth, sugar, and opium. Kidd sold most of this valuable stolen cargo on India's southwestern coast, netting about seven thousand British pounds—a small fortune during this era. He sold the rest of the cargo at the island of Hispaniola in the Caribbean Sea. Then he sailed for Boston in the British North American colony of Massachusetts. By then a wanted man, Kidd was arrested in Boston. He tried to convince the colony's British governor that he was still a licensed privateer and not a pirate. Not persuaded, the governor sent Kidd back to London, where he was put into a dark, cramped cell at Newgate Prison in April 1700.

Over a year later, in May 1701, Kidd went on trial in London for Moore's murder and for multiple counts of piracy. He was found guilty and hanged on the gallows outside Newgate, with a large crowd of Londoners in attendance. Officials then chained his lifeless body to a post on the shore of the city's River Thames. All who passed recognized the display as a fearsome warning to would-be pirates.

Kidd's legend has lived on in several ways. To accompany Kidd's execution, an anonymous songwriter crafted a ballad called "Captain Kidd." One of its verses says, "I murdered William Moore and I left him in his gore / Forty leagues [approximately 120 miles, or 93 kilometers] from shore, as I sailed as I sailed." That and additional verses were printed on big sheets of paper called broadsides and sold around London. The song became popular and spread by word of

Many pirates died brutally. Some were slain in battle. Those who were caught by the law were often hanged. After William Kidd was hanged in 1701, British officials displayed his dead body in London to show would-be pirates the punishment that awaited them. This engraving comes from *The Pirates Own Book* by Charles Ellms, published in 1837.

mouth, from singer to singer, throughout Britain and the American colonies. The legend of Captain Kidd also includes hidden treasure. Rumors spread that in 1699 he buried chests and bundles of loot on Gardiners Island, at the eastern end of Long Island in New York. For centuries, treasure hunters looked for Kidd's booty. Even though nobody ever found it—or proved that it had really existed—the story gave rise to the enduring myth that pirates of the Golden Age buried their treasure.

GOLD STAINED WITH CRIMSON

During the War of the Spanish Succession (1701–1714), Holland, Britain, and several German and Austrian states fought against Spain and France. At this time, privateers found their services in great demand. But when the war ended, seasoned privateers were suddenly out of work. Many British sailors were also out of a job, since Britain's Royal Navy, bankrupted by the expensive war, laid off almost three-fourths of its total manpower (thirty-six thousand men) at war's end. Thousands of unemployed sailors pleaded for work on merchant ships. With so many men desperate for work, merchant captains who did hire sailors were able to pay them drastically reduced wages—50 percent of what sailors had earned during the war. As a result, many disgruntled, unemployed sailors and privateers, with no legal way of making a living, turned to piracy.

These pirates became an international menace. Historians estimate that by 1717, between fifteen and twenty-five pirate ships, each with an average of eighty men, were operating in Caribbean and North Atlantic waters. By contrast, most of the trading ships sailing through these waters had crews of only ten to twenty men and were lightly armed. The merchant ships were no match for pirate vessels with more than double the firepower. In fact, pirate ships were generally unstoppable by any craft less powerful than a naval warship.

JOLLY ROGER

Life aboard any ship in the eighteenth century—whether a pirate ship, a merchant ship, or a naval ship—was rough and dirty. Ships carried a limited supply of clean drinking water, and what freshwater they did carry was sometimes tainted with bacteria. So sailors drank a lot of alcohol, which was usually safer and cleaner than the water supply. In this era before refrigeration, ships were stocked with foods that wouldn't quickly spoil, such as salted and dried meat and hardtack, a bland-tasting biscuit. Pirates also ate fresh fish from the waters in which they sailed. Food could run low after long stretches at sea, so whenever pirates captured another ship, they eagerly took its food supplies. If they raided a ship that carried cattle as cargo, for example, they killed the animals for meat. Fresh fruits and vegetables were rare aboard pirate ships, and without the vitamin C contained in these foods, pirates could develop scurvy, a painful disease of the gums, skin, and bloodstream.

Pirate raids and battles were extremely bloody. To capture a cargo ship, pirates frequently began by firing a single cannon shot across its bow (front), a move that often persuaded the merchant captain to surrender immediately. But if the opponent—such as a naval ship or a privateer—was up for a fight, crews would engage each other in hand-to-hand combat. First, pirates tossed grappling hooks—multipronged hooks attached to ropes—onto the enemy ship, snagging it and using the ropes to pull the two vessels together. Then the pirates scrambled aboard the opposing vessel, and men on both sides attacked each other with muskets, pistols, axes, swords, and daggers. The crews also continued to fire at each other with cannons. One buccaneer described the outcome of a pirate raid on three Spanish ships in 1680, writing about one stricken vessel: "Such a miserable sight I never saw in my life, for not one man there was found but was either killed, desperately wounded, or horribly burnt with [gun]powder." On a second ship, "blood ran down the decks in whole streams, scarce one place in the ship was found that was free from blood."

Even without raids and battles, life on a pirate ship could be dangerous. Ships were often caught in life-threatening storms, and handling ropes and other heavy equipment during turbulent weather left many pirates with painful injuries and scars. In the days before antibiotics and other modern medical treatments, wounds could easily become infected, leading to a pirate's death. It wasn't uncommon to see pirates with missing arms or legs. Sometimes cannonballs had blown off the limbs. In other cases, a wounded arm or leg had to be sawed off to prevent death by infection.

When pirates weren't fighting, their lives could be orderly and sometimes even democratic. Nobody could join a pirate crew without either swearing an oath or signing a document called the pirate articles. The articles detailed the way a particular pirate crew dealt with such matters as discipline and the sharing of pirate loot. (The captain usually got the largest share, and the rest was divided among the crew.) The articles were the laws of the ship, and they varied from crew to crew. On some ships, pirates took votes to elect their captain and to decide other matters.

Pirate crews of this era were usually a mixture of nationalities. For instance, in 1717 pirates on Samuel Bellamy's ship included men from all over northern Europe, as well as American Indians and Africans. This diverse pirate alliance fit well with many pirates' notions of themselves as men without a country. Pirates frequently were angry with rulers, governors, and other authority figures in the nations of their birth, who often treated working-class people poorly. Naval and merchant sea captains were famous for bullying and abusing sailors on their ships. For example, in 1734 a merchant seaman named Richard Baker fell ill during a voyage and was unable to come on deck when his captain called him. As a punishment, the captain whipped Baker and tied him to one of the ship's masts, where he hung for more than an hour. Baker died a few days later. Sometimes captains beat crewmen with iron bars and boat hooks. Many sailors became pirates to escape such sadistic captains. In fact, the crews of merchant ships were often so unhappy with their treatment that when attacked by pirates, a portion of the crew willingly joined the pirates' ranks.

"EVERY MAN HAS A VOTE IN AFFAIRS OF MOMENT; HAS EQUAL TITLE TO THE FRESH PROVISIONS [FOOD], OR STRONG LIQUORS, AT ANY TIME SEIZED, & USE OF THEM AT PLEASURE, UNLESS A SCARCITY MAKE IT NECESSARY, FOR THE GOOD OF ALL, TO VOTE A RETRENCHMENT [REDUCTION]."

—excerpt from *Royal Fortune*'s pirate articles, Bartholomew Roberts, captain, 1720

THE REMARKABLE DEATH OF WILLIAM FLY

Many pirates are remembered for how they lived. William Fly is most memorable for how he died. On July 12, 1726, when Fly stood on the gallows in Boston, Massachusetts, to be hanged for his crimes as a pirate, he noticed that the noose prepared to hang him hadn't been tied properly. As an experienced sailor, Fly was an expert in tying knots in ropes, so he sat the hangman down, showed him the proper method, and retied the knot himself.

He then addressed the crowd that had assembled to see him hang. It was filled with many sailors and sea captains. He scolded the captains, saying that they should pay their sailors a fair wage and treat them better. Fly explained that when he had been a sailor, barbaric treatment by his captain had pushed him to become a pirate. The executioner then placed the properly tied rope around Fly's neck and hanged him.

The typical pirate flag, called a Jolly Roger, was made of black cloth displaying a white skull and crossbones. This image reflected the defiant attitude of piracy. And many pirate ships of the Golden Age had the word *revenge* as part of their names. Pirates felt that by attacking naval and merchant ships, they were enacting vengeance on an unjust society.

BLACKBEARD: MAN OR MONSTER?

Edward Teach, more commonly known as Blackbeard, was a flamboyant pirate of the Golden Age. Teach liked to place a lighted, slow-burning match or fuse (the kind used to fire a cannon) under his hat. The fire would produce a trail of smoke, seemingly coming from Teach's head, cloaking him in a perpetual fog and making him look like the devil. That's the effect that Teach desired—he wanted his foes to think he was a demon.

This illustration from the 1750s shows Blackbeard with lit fuses beneath his hat. The pirate known as Edward Teach wanted to create a devilish appearance to frighten his foes.

Teach understood the importance of cultivating a deadly reputation and making himself seem more monstrous than he actually was. The flag on his ship displayed a white horned skeleton holding a spear pointing to a bloody red heart.

As with many Golden Age pirates, historians know little about Teach's early life and true identity. They know that Edward Teach was a pirate but aren't even sure of his real name. This is largely because many pirates assumed aliases to hide from the law. So the name Edward Teach (Edward Thatch is also sometimes recorded) might be a pseudonym.

Historians do know that when Teach was a young man, during the War of the Spanish Succession, he was a privateer, serving on a vessel based in Jamaica. Britain's Queen Anne had authorized his ship to plunder French and Spanish vessels. By the end of the war, Teach had turned pirate, joining up with a crew of Caribbean pirates led by Captain Benjamin Hornigold.

Hornigold saw much potential in his young apprentice and eventually gave Teach command of his own stolen vessel. Working together, Hornigold and Teach were quite successful. However, Hornigold was a wanted man and eventually agreed to a deal issued by Britain's King George I: if Hornigold walked away from the pirate life immediately, all charges against him would be dropped. With Hornigold going straight, Teach set out on his own. He embarked on a lone reign of terror that lasted from 1717 to 1718.

THE SAILOR AND THE DEMON

In the autumn of 1718, by then known as Blackbeard, Teach sailed to a favorite hideaway on Ocracoke Island off the coast of North Carolina. There he enjoyed a wild get-together with many of his pirate friends. The pirates danced, sang, and drank. Alexander Spotswood, the governor of Virginia (another British North America colony), heard about the pirate party and decided that this was the perfect chance to put a stop to the infamous Blackbeard. If he planned it carefully enough, Spotswood hoped, he could catch Blackbeard unawares and corner the fearsome pirate at Ocracoke.

After several weeks of planning, Spotswood sent two sloops to Ocracoke. Both were commanded by Royal Navy lieutenant Robert Maynard. When Blackbeard saw the navy's sails on the horizon, he realized he was trapped. But instead of trying to outrun the navy sloops, Blackbeard led them on a chase through a narrow channel between the beach and a barely noticeable sandbar. As Blackbeard had planned, the sloops crashed into the sandbar. It looked as if Blackbeard was home free—until his ship slammed into a sandbar.

One of Maynard's sloops was demolished. The crew managed to free the other from the sandbar. On this ship, Maynard urged his men to hide below deck. With his vessel appearing to be nearly empty of crew members, Maynard made a beeline for Blackbeard's ship.

Once the naval sloop was close enough, Blackbeard and his men boarded it. Suddenly they were ambushed by Maynard's full crew, who sprang out and rushed the deck, pistols ablaze. With much of his crew defeated, Blackbeard aimed a pistol at Maynard, who aimed his pistol back at Blackbeard. Both men fired. Blackbeard missed. Maynard didn't, but his bullet only wounded Blackbeard. Several of Maynard's men then joined in to attack the pirate. According to legend, it took five musket-ball shots and twenty sword thrusts to finally kill Blackbeard. As a gory message to all other pirates in the area, Maynard ordered Blackbeard's head cut off and suspended from the bow of his ship.

SLAVES, PIRATES, AND AFRICAN CHIEFS

The Golden Age of Piracy coincided with the peak years of the Atlantic slave trade, when millions of Africans were captured in their homelands, transported across the Atlantic Ocean in chains, and sold to plantation owners in the Americas. During this period, some pirates were involved in the capture, sale, and transport of slaves. They treated African captives like any other cargo to be bought and sold. Other pirates sided with the slaves. For instance, after robbing a slave ship, some pirates unshackled the slaves and let them murder the ship's crew. Occasionally, pirates took the captives ashore and set them free. Some pirate crews welcomed freed captives into their ranks.

African American historian Henry Louis Gates Jr. notes that many seventeenth- and eighteenth-century pirates were black. A white captive on Bartholomew Roberts's ship reported in 1721 that Roberts's crew was made up of "250 [white] Men and 50 Negroes." In 1718, 60 percent of Blackbeard's crew was composed of black pirates. Historical documents mention three pirates nicknamed el Mulato. *Mulatto* is an outdated word for a person with both white and black

Pirates often encountered ships loaded with African captives on the Atlantic Ocean. Sometimes pirates took control of the ships and sold the captives at slave markets in the Americas. Other times pirates freed the slaves. Some captives even joined pirate crews. This engraving of slaves on a ship bound for the Americas dates to 1860.

ancestry, especially someone with one black parent and one white parent. So all three "el Mulato" pirates probably were biracial. Two other pirates were known as Black Caesar, one of whom was said to be a former African chief.

Because records from this period are relatively sparse, it is difficult to know exactly how black men were treated on pirate ships. Historians believe that some black pirates were forced into a servile role, similar to slavery. Others were free, full-fledged crew members. Historians also say that no matter what their status, black men serving on pirate crews had more rights than they would have had almost anywhere else in white society at this time. And black pirates received their fair share of pirate booty and enjoyed other rights guaranteed to pirates, such as the right to vote on matters concerning the crew.

UNLADYLIKE PIRATES

Before the twentieth century, women in most of the world had very few legal rights. A British law book from 1632 mentions that "women have nothing to do in constituting Lawes, or consenting to them, in interpreting of Lawes, or in hearing them interpreted." By law, most women of this era could not vote, own property, or make financial decisions. They were usually subservient to their fathers or husbands. Other than an officer's wife, it was rare to find a woman on a merchant or naval vessel during this era. Yet a few women became pirates, and they offer some of the more colorful stories from the Golden Age of Piracy.

Two famed female pirates sailed with Calico Jack Rackam, whose nickname came from his preference for bright clothing made from Indian calico cloth. Rackam operated in the seas around Jamaica in the early eighteenth century, looting local trading vessels and small fishing boats. Rackam was considered a minor pirate during this era. He is largely remembered not for his years as a pirate captain but for his relationships with the female pirates Anne Bonny and Mary Read.

Rackam met Bonny in the Bahamas in 1719. He was there to accept a pardon offered to pirates by Woodes Rogers, the British governor of the Bahamas. Once pardoned, Rackam briefly retired from piracy.

THE IRISH PIRATE QUEEN

The earliest known female pirate was Grace O'Malley, born in Connaught, Ireland, in 1530. Known as the Irish Pirate Queen, O'Malley took command of her father's fishing and trading ships after he died. For several decades, her fleet attacked British merchant ships and raided villages that cooperated with the British government, which at the time ruled Ireland oppressively. In the 1580s, the British fought back against O'Malley, capturing her fleet and taking her son hostage. O'Malley died at Rockfleet Castle, her home on the western coast of Ireland, in 1603.

Dressed in men's clothing, Anne Bonny worked as a pirate alongside Mary Read and Calico Jack Rackam. Victims reported that the two female pirates were just as bloodthirsty as their male companions. This engraving is from a 1725 Dutch edition of Daniel Defoe's *A General History of the Pyrates*.

He then met Bonny, who was married to a former pirate. He convinced her to abandon her husband and to go to sea with him. Rackam reentered the pirate's life, and Bonny joined him, dressing herself in men's clothing.

Many British folk songs tell of young women going to sea disguised as men, dressed in sailors' clothing. Mary Read was apparently one such woman. According to Daniel Defoe's *A General History of the Pyrates*, Read, dressed as a sailor, was taken prisoner when her vessel was conquered by Jack Rackam. The story says that Anne Bonny, by then sailing with Rackam, tried to seduce this handsome young "gentleman." Read bared her breasts, exposing herself to Bonny as a woman. Bonny promised to keep Read's secret. Many historians doubt the specifics of Defoe's tale. What is true, however, is that Read joined Rackam and Bonny to lead a pirate's life herself.

All three were back in the Bahamas by the summer of 1720, when they stole a sloop named the *William* from Nassau harbor. Rogers was determined to flush all pirates out of Nassau and to reestablish lawfulness there. When Rogers heard that the *William* had been taken, he began a hunt for Rackam and his crew. A privateer named Jonathan Barnet, licensed by the governor of Jamaica to arrest pirates, captured Rackam, Bonny, and Read when they showed up in Negril Point, Jamaica, fleeing from Rogers's forces. Barnet delivered them to the jail in Spanish Town, Jamaica, where they were tried in November 1720 for piracy.

During the trial, witnesses asserted that Bonny and Read had committed crimes, including the raiding and theft of many schooners and sloops, just as viciously as their male coconspirator. One witness testified that "the two women . . . wore men's jackets, and long trousers, and handkerchiefs tied about their heads . . . each of them had a machet[e] and pistol in their hands, and cursed and swore at the men [of Rackam's crew], to murder the [witness]. For their crimes, the three were found guilty and sentenced to death by hanging.

The judge asked if there was any reason the punishment should not be carried out. As Defoe wrote in *A General History of the Pyrates*, "Both of them pleaded their bellies, being quick with child [pregnant], and pray'd that execution might be staid." Pleading pregnancy was a sure way to avoid execution, because no court at that time would take the life of an unborn child by executing its mother.

When a doctor confirmed that each woman was indeed pregnant, Bonny and Read were spared the hangman's rope. Read contracted a fever and died in prison shortly afterward. Bonny survived, but nobody knows for certain what happened to her or her child. Calico Jack Rackam was executed.

THE DREAD PIRATE ROBERTS

One of the most successful—and fiercest—pirates in the Golden Age was Bartholomew Roberts, also known as Black Bart. Born John Roberts in Wales in 1682, he served on British merchant ships during the War of the Spanish Succession. After the war, he worked on a slave ship called the *Princess*. In 1719 pirates attacked the *Princess* and forced Roberts to join them in piracy.

CLOTHES MAKE THE PIRATE

When they plundered a ship, pirates often stole the fine clothes of the captain and other officers. So pirates sometimes wore fashionable clothing of the era, such as long coats and tricornered hats with feathered plumes. Pirate Bartholomew Roberts was known for his flashy fashion sense. On the day he died, Roberts was supposedly decked out from head to toe entirely in crimson, with a red feather in his hat and gold chains around his neck, the latter accented by a diamond cross.

This engraving shows Bartholomew Roberts in the flashy clothing he allegedly wore when he met his death. This woodcut of Roberts dates to 1725.

Renaming himself Bartholomew, Roberts quickly embraced the pirate's life. He was widely quoted as saying, "In an honest service [job], there is thin victuals [meager food], low wages and hard labour. In this [piracy], plenty . . . pleasure and ease, liberty and power, . . . No, a merry life and a short one shall be my motto."

During his three-year pirating career, Roberts captured more than four hundred vessels. He could be sadistic, sometimes hanging captured sailors from yardarms (posts affixed to a ship's mast) and allowing his pirates to use the victims for target practice. Many sailors knew of his viciousness and surrendered their ships to him without a fight. However, in 1720 a well-armed Dutch vessel chose to resist Roberts, so Black Bart's crew swarmed the Dutch ship, mutilating everyone on board. The pirates cut off the Dutch captain's ears and presented them to him as a reminder to listen harder when Bartholomew Roberts gave him an order.

Roberts's raiding of cargo ships did severe financial damage to British merchants, so the British sent a warship called the *Swallow*, captained by Challoner Ogle, to stop him. In 1722 the *Swallow* caught up with Roberts near Cape Lopez in what is now Gabon in West Africa. The *Swallow* blasted Black Bart with roaring cannon fire, and Roberts was fatally wounded. His crew tossed the body overboard, in accordance with his wishes for a burial at sea.

THE END OF AN AGE

With the end of the War of the Spanish Succession, British authorities decided to clean up the pirate problem in the Caribbean Sea. In the 1720s, the British navy increased patrols in pirate-ridden areas. The British government also offered rewards for the capture of pirates—an incentive to citizens and privateers alike to help flush out pirates in hiding. And Britain licensed extra privateers specifically to capture pirates. Some of these privateers were former pirates themselves, so they knew where pirates might be hiding and what tactics pirates might use to evade capture. In some areas, the British government offered pirates pardons. Under these deals, if the pirates agreed to go straight, they would not be prosecuted for their former crimes. In other cases, pirates were put on trial and often executed. By 1726 only two hundred pirates were operating in the Caribbean and the North Atlantic—down from an estimated twelve hundred to two thousand a decade earlier. The Golden Age of Piracy had ended.

CHAPTER THREE

FROM SABERS TO ROCKET LAUNCHERS

By the late eighteenth century, the Golden Age of Piracy was just a faint memory. But pirates still operated in other parts of the world.

Along the coast of North Africa, the states of Morocco, Tunis, Tripoli, and Algiers (called the Barbary States) sent corsairs to attack European shipping vessels on the Mediterranean. The corsairs not only captured cargoes of silk, cotton, grain, spices, and other goods, but they frequently also kidnapped seamen. Sometimes, the corsairs demanded hefty ransoms from the sailors' families or governments for their return. Sometimes they sold the captives into slavery in North Africa.

To keep their ships safe, many of the ruling powers of Europe chose to sign treaties with the Barbary States. Under these agreements, European nations paid tribute, or large sums of money, to Barbary governments. In exchange, the Barbary States agreed not to attack European trading vessels on the Mediterranean.

THE BARBARY WARS

Britain had such an agreement with the Barbary governments. The money it paid not only kept British ships sailing from England safe but also protected ships sailing from Britain's American colonies. In 1783, however, the United States officially gained its independence from Great Britain. No longer protected by Britain's international agreements or Britain's powerful navy, American merchant ships were suddenly vulnerable to attacks from Barbary corsairs.

US trade goods included tobacco, cotton, sugar, and lumber, and Mediterranean trade routes were important to US financial prosperity. To keep this trade flourishing, the first two US presidents, George Washington and John Adams, agreed to pay the large tributes demanded by the Barbary governments.

By the time Thomas Jefferson became president in 1801, Barbary tribute prices were skyrocketing. Jefferson made the bold move of refusing to give in to Tripoli's demands for tribute. In response, Yusuf Karamanli, the pasha (ruler) of Tripoli, declared war on the United States in May 1801. Jefferson sent a squad of naval vessels against Tripoli, and four years of war followed. Under a peace treaty, the US government paid ransom money for the release of US sailors held captive in Tripoli, but the United States would no longer have to pay tribute to Tripoli. The United States sent forces to the Barbary Coast again in 1815, this time to defeat Algiers. After this war, the Barbary rulers agreed to stop raiding US merchant ships.

THE MOST SUCCESSFUL PIRATE IN HISTORY

During the first half of the nineteenth century, China was home to perhaps the most successful pirate in history—a woman known as Cheng I Sao. Little is known about her early life, including her birth name. Historians do know that before she was a pirate, she was a prostitute known for her beauty and toughness. After she married a Chinese pirate leader named Cheng in 1801, she took the name Cheng I Sao, which means "wife of Cheng."

US naval commander Stephen Decatur, a hero of the Barbary Wars (1801–1805 and 1815–1816), fought to defeat North African pirates on the Mediterranean Sea. In this painting by Dennis Malone Carter from 1878, Decatur and his men attack the crew of a gunboat from the state of Tripoli.

She agreed to the marriage on one condition: that she become an equal partner in her husband's piracy business. Cheng agreed, and over the next six years, this husband-and-wife pirate team expanded their wealth and created an alliance of pirates from competing Chinese clans. After Cheng died in 1807, his wife refused to recede into the background, as was expected of most women during that era. Instead, she became the sole leader of her late husband's ever-growing band of seafaring thieves.

Realizing that many of Cheng's pirate associates wouldn't accept having a woman in charge, she shrewdly made her husband's second-in-command, Chang Pao, the official captain of her fleet of pirate ships. Meanwhile, Cheng I Sao concentrated on military strategy and business dealings.

Eventually, Cheng I Sao controlled almost all the piracy on the South China Sea. She commanded a fleet of more than fifteen hundred ships and more than eighty thousand sailors. Known as the Red Flag Fleet—for the color of her ships' banners—her pirate band was bigger

Cheng I Sao is shown here battling an enemy with a sword. At her height of power, she commanded a fleet of fifteen hundred ships and tens of thousands of pirates. This illustration appeared in a book written by Yuentsze-yung-lun on the history of Chinese pirates (1810).

than the navies of most countries. Her pirate crews pillaged boats of all sizes, from tiny cargo ships to imperial war vessels. She also expanded her criminal enterprises to include a protection racket. Under this arrangement, ships traveling on the South China Sea had to give her regularly scheduled payments. In return, they would be assured safe passage. If they didn't pay, her pirates would steal their cargo.

In 1809 Cheng I Sao's fleet repelled attacks by the Chinese navy, which was determined to put an end to her reign. In desperation, the Chinese government hired Portuguese and British naval forces to help capture Cheng I Sao. The European ships were heavily armed and staffed with trained sailors, but they were powerless to defeat her well-organized and enormous fleet. So in 1810, the Chinese government instead tried to lure her with a pardon if she would give up her criminal activities. Cheng I Sao was a shrewd negotiator. She struck a great deal with the government. A few hundred of her men were exiled from China. More than one hundred were executed for their crimes. Thousands more had to surrender their boats and weapons but got to keep all the loot they had stolen. Some of them even got jobs in the Chinese military. Cheng I Sao held up her end of the bargain, retiring from her life of crime. She opened a gambling house in Canton and died peacefully at the age of sixty-nine in 1844.

THE PIRATE OF LAKE MICHIGAN

Most historical pirates made their living on the high seas, but Dan Seavey did his pirating on the Great Lakes, a chain of five lakes in the center of North America. Seavey, who was born in Maine in 1865, started his working life as a sailor in the US Navy. After a failed attempt to get rich during the Alaskan gold rush of the late 1890s, he was broke, with a schooner dubbed the *Wanderer* among his only possessions. That's when he turned to piracy. He brought a cannon on board the *Wanderer* and sailed the Great Lakes, stealing alcohol, venison, and other goods from ships and selling this cargo at port cities.

One of Seavey's signature moves was moon cussing, which involved moving lamps set up by the authorities to help ships navigate on the Great Lakes at night. The misplaced lights sent ships off course toward rocky coasts. Many boats got stuck on the rocks or ran aground in shallow waters, where they were easy prey for Seavey, who awaited them there to steal their cargo.

Seavey is best known for a feat he pulled off in 1908, when he captured the schooner *Nellie Johnson* at a dock in Grand Haven, Michigan, on the Lake Michigan coast. He came aboard armed with nothing but liquor and invited the ship's crew to have a few drinks with him. Somehow he stayed fairly sober (either because he had an enormous tolerance for alcohol or by merely pretending to drink), while the crew got completely drunk. Seavey then tossed unsteady sailors out of their own ship and singlehandedly sailed the *Nellie Johnson* to Chicago, Illinois, where he sold the ship's cargo of valuable cedar wood posts.

After leaving Chicago, Seavey realized that a US deputy marshal was in hot pursuit, aboard the US Revenue Cutter Service vessel *Tuscarora*. By then Seavey had hidden the *Nellie Johnson* on a nearby river and was back in the *Wanderer*. When the *Tuscarora* approached, Seavey surrendered without any fuss. Newspapers of the day embellished the event considerably, writing that the *Tuscarora* hit Seavey's boat with a cannon shot and that a team of armed lawmen boarded the *Wanderer*.

Even though the real incident wasn't quite so exciting, Seavey was indeed arrested. He went on trial in Chicago for the *Nellie Johnson* heist, but the judge set him free. The details of the trial are lost, but historians say that Seavey's lawyer might have pulled strings in Chicago's legal community to get him freed.

ONE OF SEAVEY'S SIGNATURE MOVES WAS MOON CUSSING, WHICH INVOLVED MOVING LAMPS SET UP BY THE AUTHORITIES TO HELP SHIPS NAVIGATE ON THE GREAT LAKES AT NIGHT.

When pirate Dan Seavey looted ships on the Great Lakes, the job of stopping him fell to the US Revenue Cutter Service (which later became the US Coast Guard). This Revenue Cutter Service ship, the *Perry*, patrolled Lake Erie during the era when Seavey was active.

PIRATES WITH ROCKET LAUNCHERS

During the twentieth century, with powerful, well-armed navies sailing the world's seas, few people tried to make a living by piracy. Most pirates appeared only in films and books. But by the end of the century, real-life pirates were in the news. In 1991 rebels overthrew the government of Somalia in northeastern Africa. The country fell into turmoil, with power split among heavily armed rival clans. The nation managed to set up a weak central government, but it had no coast guard to protect its fishing grounds. Ships from Europe and Asia started fishing illegally in Somali waters, making off with large amounts of tuna, barracuda, and red snapper. This illegal fishing took vital business away from Somali fishers.

Some Somalis felt they needed to take vigilante action—that is, to take the law into their own hands. They organized armed gangs to keep foreign ships from fishing illegally in Somali waters. Over time, however, these gangs started hijacking huge commercial ships sailing through the Gulf of Aden north of Somalia. The gangs held the crews and cargo hostage, demanding millions of dollars in ransom from the companies that owned the ships. These were no longer vigilante groups defending Somali shores. They had become pirates.

About twenty-five thousand commercial ships pass through the Gulf of Aden every year. Some of these vessels are unarmed, so they are easy targets for pirates. Somali pirates are equipped with global positioning systems, satellite phones, rocket launchers, and machine guns. They sail in tiny motorboats called skiffs, which are too small to be detected by cargo ships' radar systems. The pirates usually attack at night, scrambling up the sides of the big boats with the help of grappling hooks, ropes, and lightweight ladders.

The pirates are mostly poor former fishers, but the bosses behind the operations are powerful and often wealthy Somali warlords and arms smugglers. The bosses provide boats, weapons, and navigational equipment to the pirates. In exchange, individual pirates get a cut of the ransom money. Between 2005 and 2012, the average ransom taken by pirates was $2.7 million per ship, and individual pirates could earn more than $30,000 per job. Some in Somalia see piracy as a noble profession, because pirates bring money back to poor communities. Piracy provides a much higher income than fishing, and pirates spend this money at home and use it to help their families survive.

A crew of Somali pirates made headlines in April 2009 when they attacked the US cargo ship *Maersk Alabama*, which was headed for Somalia, Uganda, and Kenya. The freighter's crew fought back,

Two Somali pirates sit with machine guns in a motorized skiff on the shore of the Indian Ocean. Somali pirates have carried out numerous hijackings since the 1990s. They take cargo ships and crews hostage and demand millions of dollars for their release.

stabbing one of the pirates with an ice pick and taking him hostage. The pirates took Captain Richard Phillips captive, and the two groups agreed to a hostage exchange. The pirates didn't hold up their end of the bargain, however, and set off with Phillips in one of the ship's lifeboats. They hoped to exchange Phillips for a large ransom, but the US military sent in a team of Navy SEALs, an elite commando unit, which overpowered the pirates and freed Phillips.

SOUTH CHINA SEA PIRACY VERSION 2.0

Modern-day pirates continue to make the news. During the spring and the summer of 2014, pirates traveling in fishing vessels and other boats masterminded a rash of hijackings in the South China Sea. At least eight hijackings had been reported by July 2014. Armed with handguns and machetes, the pirates boarded tanker ships—boats transporting huge amounts of valuable diesel fuel and gasoline.

The pirates siphoned the fuel from the tanks and piped it into other boats waiting nearby. Then they sailed off and vanished. No one knows where they went, who they are, or what they did with the fuel. Nobody was hurt during these heists. However, during one hijacking off the coast of Malaysia, on April 23, 2014, the pirates kidnapped three Indonesian crew members of a Japanese tanker. The men have not been heard from since. In that heist, the pirates stole roughly 792,000 gallons (3 million liters) of diesel fuel, pumping it into two waiting ships. During another tanker heist, the pirates dressed in black, ninja-style costumes. Authorities from the Malaysian Maritime Enforcement Agency are still searching for the pirates. Their identities and whereabouts remain a mystery.

DIGITAL PIRACY

Piracy is primarily defined as robbery or plundering at sea. However, the term can also refer to the unauthorized copying, distributing, and selling of creative works. In the twenty-first century, this type of piracy often happens online, when computer users illegally download and distribute movies, music, and other artworks without permission of the works' creators. One analyst estimates that online piracy costs the US film industry more than $400 million per year. Around the world, private and government organizations work to detect and shut down online piracy and to prosecute perpetrators.

CHAPTER FOUR

POP CULTURE PIRATES

The Golden Age of Piracy may have ended long ago, but the pirate legend has never died. In fact, over the past three centuries, Golden Age pirates have proved an inspiration to authors, musicians, filmmakers, TV executives, animators, and playwrights.

Most fictional pirates are more than mere villains. They are often symbols of the underdog, the nonconformist, the rugged vigilante hero. An early English-language example is the character Arviragus in Charles Johnson's *The Successful Pyrate.* The play, which debuted in London in 1713, is loosely based on the life of the real pirate Henry Avery. Although a criminal, Arviragus (the Avery character) is depicted as brave, honorable, and loyal to his pirate crew. Eventually he retires from his life of crime.

Pirates received a comic treatment more than 150 years later in the operetta *The Pirates of Penzance* (1879), created by the famed British comic opera team of W. S. Gilbert (who wrote the dialogue and lyrics) and Arthur Sullivan (who wrote the music). The story is about naive Frederic, whose nanny, mishearing Frederic's father's instructions, had many years before apprenticed him to a pirate instead of to a ship's pilot. Specifically, he was apprenticed to the Pirate King, leader of the Pirates of Penzance. This comical band of pirates never harms orphans. Their captives, knowing this, all claim to be orphans, so the pirates naively let them go.

When his apprenticeship is over, Frederic wants to become a law-abiding citizen and rid the seas of these pirates. But he is torn, because he still feels a sense of allegiance to them. The outrageous plot and exaggerated characters allow for quite a bit of slapstick comedy and funny, memorable tunes. The Pirate King in particular has some humorous dialogue, as when he defends his life as a pirate: "I don't think much of our profession, but contrasted with respectability, it is comparatively honest." The operetta was enormously popular and is still performed often in the twenty-first century.

THE SEAFARING MAN WITH ONE LEG

A few years after *The Pirates of Penzance*, a truly great literary work about pirates emerged. This was *Treasure Island*, written in 1883 by Scottish author Robert Louis Stevenson.

The story had its roots in August and September 1881, when Stevenson; his parents; his American wife, Fanny; and her twelve-year-old stepson, Lloyd, stayed together at a rented holiday cottage in Braemar, Scotland. The weather was ghastly, and the five of them tried to find ways to pass the time and to ignore the howling wind and pouring rain. Lloyd had brought a box of watercolors with him, and one afternoon, he began painting. Stevenson joined him and drew a map of an island. In the top right-hand corner of the map, he scribbled a name that promised adventure and intrigue: Treasure Island. Lloyd was enthralled.

The map inspired Stevenson to write *Treasure Island*. While he was crafting it, Lloyd and Stevenson's parents occasionally gave him plot and character ideas, which he then incorporated into the book's narrative. Stevenson's tale is about Jim Hawkins, a British child who becomes a cabin boy on a ship called the *Hispaniola*. In an inaccurate

Robert Louis Stevenson's *Treasure Island* has delighted young readers since the 1880s. The book's protagonist, Jim Hawkins, goes to sea as a cabin boy and ends up searching for pirates' treasure. This illustration appears in a 1915 edition of the book, illustrated by Louis Rhead and Walter Paget.

though enduring popular fantasy, the ship's crew goes looking for a treasure chest buried by pirates on an island much like the one Stevenson had mapped out. Along the way, Jim discovers that many of the crew members, including the one-legged cook, Long John Silver, are pirates, planning a mutiny to take over the ship. When the *Hispaniola* reaches the island, a battle breaks out between the pirates and the honest crew members, all of whom are searching for the treasure. Eventually Silver's men betray him. He allies himself with Jim and the other honest men. They secure the treasure, load it into the ship, and sail away, marooning the remaining pirates on the island.

They return to Britain safely, but the experience haunts Jim forever.

Stevenson found that the story came to him easily, and he wrote it quickly and confidently. The narrative of *Treasure Island* charges forth at a breakneck pace, and the story boasts fascinating, colorful characters, an atmospheric tone, inventive plot twists, authentic maritime and sailing details, and a relatable protagonist in young Jim Hawkins. The bond between Long John Silver and Jim is touching, and Silver eventually proves to be honorable—in his own way.

Treasure Island did not appear as a book initially. As was common with fiction in the nineteenth century, the story was first published in weekly installments, in *Young Folks* magazine, from October 1881 to January 1882. At first those issues of *Young Folks* didn't sell any more copies than usual. This changed when all the chapters were collected in a book in 1883. The novel was immediately successful on all fronts: it sold many copies, was praised by literary critics, and was admired by Stevenson's fellow authors. Britain's prime minister, William Gladstone, was rumored to have stayed up until two in the morning to finish it.

Treasure Island was Stevenson's first true success as a novelist, and it was destined to become a classic. The story has been adapted to different mediums, and its characters have appeared in TV and radio shows, musical works, and video games. For example, in 1950 Walt Disney Productions released a film version of *Treasure Island*, featuring actor Robert Newton as Long John Silver. In 1996 Kermit the Frog, Fozzie Bear, and the rest of the Muppets puppet gang appeared in the film *Muppet Treasure Island*. In 2002 Disney released *Treasure Planet*, an animated science-fiction movie in which Long John Silver is a cyborg.

THE SEAFARING MAN WITH ONE HAND

Long John Silver is missing a leg while another iconic pirate is missing a hand. His name is Captain Hook, a creation of J. M. Barrie, a

Scottish writer who admired *Treasure Island*. Barrie introduced Captain Hook in a 1904 stage play called *Peter Pan*. He later adapted the play into his 1911 novel *Peter and Wendy*.

Barrie's stage play concerns a mischievous, eternally young boy named Peter Pan. Peter can fly, and he often swoops in to eavesdrop on the Darling family in London. One night he is spotted. He ends up taking the Darling children—Wendy, John, and Michael—to Neverland, a fantastical island filled with adventure and intrigue.

At an area of Neverland known as Mermaids' Lagoon, Peter and his companions, the Lost Boys, save Tiger Lily, an American Indian princess, from the handsome and dastardly Captain Hook and his band of pirates. One of Hook's hands is missing, having been bitten off by a crocodile years earlier. The pirate has a hook on the end of his arm instead.

Eventually, Hook captures the Darling siblings and the Lost Boys, and Peter heads to Hook's pirate ship, the *Jolly Roger*. Peter battles the pirates and frees the children. In the end, Peter kicks Captain Hook into the jaws of the crocodile that had long before bitten off his hand. Wendy brings her brothers and the Lost Boys back to London, where Mrs. Darling agrees to adopt the Lost Boys. But Peter decides to stay in Neverland, where he'll remain a child forever.

Although *Peter Pan* is not exclusively a story about pirates—and the pirates don't show up until well into the tale—Captain Hook is still one of the book's most memorable characters. He comes off as a bit clownish, and Barrie made him this way on purpose. After all, *Peter Pan* is first and foremost a story for children, and the villain in a children's book isn't always exceptionally threatening. But Barrie did take pains to connect Hook to real-life historical pirates. The story tells us that prior to having his own ship, Hook worked as a boatswain, a ship's officer in charge of equipment, for Blackbeard. Hook's ship, the *Jolly Roger* (named for the pirate flag), is moored in Kidd's Creek, named for the real-life pirate Captain Kidd. And that Captain Hook is missing

Captain Hook as shown in the animated 1953 film *Peter Pan* wasn't all that scary. Such depictions helped create the modern-day image of pirates as lovable rogues, even though the truth was far different.

a hand is somewhat realistic, since it was not uncommon for real-life Golden Age pirates to lose a hand or a foot in battle.

Peter Pan has endured through the decades. In 1953 Disney released it as an animated movie. The play was turned into a Broadway musical in 1954, and in the years since, the show has been revived numerous times. A film called *Pan*, scheduled for a 2015 release, promises to tell a bit more about Captain Hook. Blackbeard himself will appear in the movie, played by Australian actor Hugh Jackman.

THE SILVER SCREEN

Not long after the US movie industry emerged in the early twentieth century, filmmakers started to make pirate movies. These films featured replicas of sloops and Spanish galleons (square-rigged ships), colorful

TERRY AND THE PIRATES

Pirates have shown up in just about every entertainment medium. During the 1930s, before the birth of television, kids followed many of their favorite action heroes on radio shows and in newspaper comics. A comic strip called *Terry and the Pirates*, launched in 1934, was set not in the Golden Age of Piracy but in mid-twentieth-century China. There, young American Terry Lee and his pals did battle with a variety of enemies, including the Dragon Lady, a beautiful pirate queen. The strip appeared in newspapers until 1946. *Terry and the Pirates* was also a popular radio serial, running from 1937 to 1948. A *Terry and the Pirates* TV show aired for one season only, in 1952 and 1953.

costumes, acrobatic sword fights, chests full of gold and jewels, and tropical island locations.

The silent film *The Black Pirate* (1926) stars the dashing Douglas Fairbanks as the Duke of Arnoldo, a young aristocrat whose father is murdered by pirates. The duke avenges his father's death by becoming a swashbuckling pirate himself and finding his father's killers. In this film, the noble-born hero becomes a pirate to correct an injustice.

In real life, few pirates came from the upper classes, but they did in movies of the mid-twentieth century. For instance, in *Captain Blood* (1935), Peter Blood (played by Errol Flynn), an upper-class physician, treats a rebel wounded in an uprising against Britain's King James II. Because he helped a rebel, Blood is labeled a traitor and sent to Port Royal, Jamaica, to be sold into slavery. Escaping bondage, he becomes a pirate. Captain Blood helped make a star out of the charismatic, handsome Errol Flynn.

Pirate movies remained popular into mid-century but then fell out of favor. As technology changed, particularly with space exploration in the 1960s and the 1970s, audiences in search of action and adventure turned away from pirate stories. They instead flocked to science-fiction epics such as *Star Wars*, which is set in a faraway galaxy.

Films such as *Captain Blood* (1935), starring Errol Flynn, made Golden Age pirates look more heroic and noble than they probably were in real life.

Superhero movies such as *Batman* (1989), which like the old pirate stories had their heroes battling injustice, were also popular.

However, some movies of the late twentieth century had minor pirate characters. For example, in the 1985 film *Goonies*, suburban kids find a treasure map that had once belonged to a pirate named One-Eyed Willie. Their discovery of the map sets the movie's plot in motion. However, pirates are far from the focal point of the film, and all the audience ever sees of One-Eyed Willie is his decayed skeleton. Similarly, the 1987 film *The Princess Bride* includes a character called the Dread Pirate Roberts, a black-suited, black-masked acrobatic buccaneer, similar in looks and manner to the pirates played by Errol Flynn in earlier decades. However, the Dread Pirate Roberts is just one of many colorful characters in a movie that has nothing to do with pirates.

BUCCANEER BUNK

Fictional pirate stories are often long on legend and short on fact. For instance, historians say that pirates never buried their treasure, as was done in *Treasure Island*. Historians also say that pirates never had victims walk the plank, as they do in *Peter Pan*. In some movies and cartoons, pirates utter phrases such as "shiver me timbers" and "yarrrrgh, me matey." Historians say that such pirate talk often involves a poor imitation of a local accent from southwestern England. It's also a parody of an accent that actor Robert Newton used in Disney's *Treasure Island* (1950) and in *Blackbeard the Pirate* (1952). That accent has been the standard for movie pirates ever since.

Pirates of pop culture are often depicted as wearing a black patch over one eye. This image gives the impression that many pirates lost an eye during sea battles—and perhaps some did. But some scientists propose a different theory. They note that it takes up to twenty-five minutes for our eyes to adjust from darkness to bright light. That would make it hard for pirates to see clearly as they moved above and below decks during raids and battles. If a pirate kept a patch over one eye and the other exposed, one eye would always be adapted to poorly lit areas below deck and the other would be adapted to sunlight. That might be true, but regardless, historians have found few examples of real pirates wearing eye patches. The eye patch, it seems, is probably another example of buccaneer bunk.

BLOCKBUSTER

Pirates of the Caribbean: Curse of the Black Pearl, released in 2003, was a game changer for pirate movies. Based on a Disneyland theme park ride, it was a big-budget special effects extravaganza starring Johnny Depp. Depp had made his name playing quirky roles in small independent movies. He was not a big action star like Tom Cruise or Brad Pitt. Casting Depp was a gamble for the filmmakers, but this gamble paid off—big time. The first *Pirates of the Caribbean* film pulled in more than $300 million in ticket sales when it appeared in US movie theaters.

Even though Golden Age pirates were criminals, many people admire them because they were tough and followed their own rules. Johnny Depp called them the rock stars of the eighteenth century. He played up this image in the *Pirates of the Caribbean* movies.

Curse of the Black Pearl is about the eccentric and charming pirate Jack Sparrow (Depp). His archenemy and former comrade, Captain Hector Barbossa (Geoffrey Rush), has stolen his ship, the *Black Pearl*. Barbossa and his men kidnap Elizabeth Swann (Keira Knightley), the daughter of the governor of Port Royal, Jamaica. Swann's childhood friend, blacksmith Will Turner (Orlando Bloom), forges an alliance with Sparrow to retrieve both the Black Pearl and Elizabeth. The two heroes commandeer a ship to pursue Barbossa's pirate crew. They in turn are pursued by Commodore James Norrington, who wants to make Swann his wife. Sparrow, Turner, and Norrington don't know that Barbossa and his crew have been cursed by a treasure that they stole many years earlier. Ever since, they've existed as the undead. Only the moonlight shows them as they really are—living skeletons. Only one thing can break the curse: the stolen treasure must be returned—every last piece of it.

Three more pirate films followed *Curse of the Black Pearl*, and a fifth installment is scheduled for 2017. All of these movies deal heavily in fantasy, with elements such as the walking dead, magical curses, sea monsters, hybrid fish-men, and other supernatural elements. Yet in some ways, they are much more realistic than the Errol Flynn or Douglas Fairbanks pirate movies. For example, the filmmakers took great pains to make Jack Sparrow and the other pirates look as disgusting as possible. Their eyes are bloodshot, their teeth yellow and grimy, their skin sunburned and leathery, and their clothes tattered and worn. This is probably what pirates in the Golden Age actually looked like. A pirate ship was not a place of hygiene and cleanliness.

These movies contain references to pirates both real and fictional. For instance, Hector Barbossa's name echoes that of real-life Ottoman pirate Hayreddin Barbarossa. And in the 2011 film *Pirates of the Caribbean: On Stranger Tides*, Barbossa (who by that point in the series has lost a leg) is referred to as the "one-legged man," in a nod to the fictional Long John Silver.

THE REAL DEAL

The 2013 film *Captain Phillips* is a far cry from the *Pirates of the Caribbean* films or any earlier pirate movies. It tells the real-life story of the hijacking of the *Maersk Alabama* and the kidnapping of Captain Richard Phillips (played by Tom Hanks) by Somali pirates in 2009. Captain Phillips himself documented the experience in a best-selling book, which was the basis for the Oscar-nominated film.

The book and the movie showed audiences that piracy is still a very real and dangerous threat. As *Washington Post* critic Ann Hornaday said in her review of *Captain Phillips*, "[Director Paul] Greengrass and screenwriter Billy Ray (*Shattered Glass*) go one step further, introducing viewers to the poverty, desperation and cynicism that converge to lead four Somali fishermen to go to work for a warlord, attacking container ships and absconding [taking off] with their cargo." The powerful 2012 Danish film *A Hijacking*, also about Somali pirates, further explored modern-day piracy.

PIRATES CONQUER TELEVISION

A few early television shows, most notably the 1956 British series *The Buccaneers*, dealt with Golden Age pirates. Otherwise, pirate-themed television shows are a relatively recent development. The mostly animated kids show *SpongeBob SquarePants*, which debuted in 1999, features several pirate characters. Painty the Pirate is a living painting of a pirate who sings the show's opening theme song. Patchy the Pirate occasionally appears in live-action segments on the show, and a green, glowing pirate ghost named the Flying Dutchman appears every so often as well.

The Disney Junior network animated series *Jake and the Never Land Pirates*, which began airing in 2011, focuses on three young children: Jake, Izzy, and Cubby. All three of them are pirates in the sense that they search for treasure. The one obstacle to their treasure-hunting adventures is Captain Hook and his crew of pirates. In this show,

Based on a true story, *Captain Phillips* (2013) stars Tom Hanks as a cargo ship captain held hostage by Somali pirates.

Hook is so buffoonish and inept—nothing like the original Captain Hook of *Peter Pan*—that Jake and his friends sometimes have to help him out so he doesn't get swallowed by a crocodile or swindled by a more capable villain.

On the adult television drama *Once Upon a Time*, which also debuted in 2011, a more complex version of Captain Hook arrived early in the second season. The show takes place in the make-believe town of Storybrooke, Maine, which is populated entirely by characters from fairy tales and fiction. They have all been sent to the real world by a magical curse. Hook entered the series as the handsome, dashing

Killian Jones, the lieutenant of a ship called the *Jewel of the Realm*. He turns to piracy and embarks on a love affair with the wife of the fairy-tale character Rumplestiltskin, igniting his wrath. Rumplestiltskin slices off Killian's hand, which Killian replaces with a hook, thereafter calling himself Captain Hook.

The year 2014 saw the debut of two pirate-themed prime-time dramas: *Black Sails* on the Starz network and *Crossbones* on NBC. Each show takes a different angle on Golden Age piracy. *Black Sails* is in some ways a prequel to the novel *Treasure Island*. In it viewers get to know the fictional Captain Flint, a character from *Treasure Island* who has already been murdered by the time the novel begins. The TV characters also include several real-life pirates, such as Benjamin Hornigold and Anne Bonny. In *Crossbones*, set in 1729 in the Caribbean islands, a British citizen has invented a device to help sailors navigate at sea. Called a chronometer (a real invention), the device will enable the British Empire to further its overseas reach and power. Without the machine, British naval ships will remain easy prey for pirates. Blackbeard (played by renowned actor John Malkovich) steals the chronometer, and the Royal Navy gives spy Tom Lowe (Richard Coyle) a mission: to pose as a ship's surgeon, earn Blackbeard's trust, wrangle the chronometer from him, and murder the legendary pirate. Of course, lots of things can and do go wrong as Lowe is carrying out his job. *Crossbones* is loosely based on the 2007 nonfiction book *The Republic of Pirates* by Colin Woodard.

BEFORE WE WALK THE PLANK

Pirate imagery and mythology are everywhere in modern culture. A chain of US seafood restaurants is called Long John Silver's. Many sports teams are named for pirates. These include the Pittsburgh Pirates baseball team, which has had various pirate logos over the decades—most of them showing a pirate in a tricornered hat, an eye patch, and a beard or stubble. The logo of the Tampa Bay Buccaneers football team is a red Jolly Roger flying from a pirate's cutlass. The Oakland Raiders, another football team, has as its logo a football-helmeted pirate wearing an eye patch, with crossed swords behind his head.

Many video games feature pirates. Among them is 2013's historical action-adventure game *Assassin's Creed IV: Black Flag*, set in the Caribbean during the early eighteenth century. The *Monkey Island* series of games also take place in the Caribbean during the Golden Age of Piracy. Writers continue to be inspired by pirates of the Golden Age. For example, the Bloody Jack series of young adult novels, by author L. A. Meyer, features the young pirate Mary "Jacky" Faber. She dresses as a boy and serves on a pirate ship.

The Tampa Bay Buccaneers' Raymond James Stadium is outfitted with a life-sized pirate ship. Located in the north end zone (also known as Buccaneer Cove), the ship is equipped with several cannons that fire confetti and more after each Buccaneer touchdown or field goal.

THE SINGING PIRATE

The 1948 movie *The Pirate* features legendary singer Judy Garland crooning about her longed-for pirate love Mack the Black. Also in the film, dressed as a pirate, costar Gene Kelly dances the dramatic "Pirate Ballet," complete with sword fights and booming cannons.

It's unlikely that real-life pirates danced and sang like Garland and Kelly, but they probably did sing onboard ship. Sailors of the Golden Age commonly sang sea shanties as they worked. These were rhythmic songs, sung in time with the strenuous tasks of hauling cargo, raising anchors, and hoisting sails. By singing in unison and syncing their movements to music, sailors made their work a little easier. A modern San Francisco singing group called Sons of the Buccaneers (SOBs) keeps this tradition alive by performing shanties and other sea songs of the Golden Age. Although shanties were not specific to pirates, the SOB website features a lot of pirate imagery, including a Jolly Roger logo and links to pirate books and merchandise.

PIRATE COOL

Most societies romanticize criminals to some extent. For instance, in gangster movies of the 1930s, the bad guys were shown to be independent-minded outsiders. They might have been criminals, but audiences admired them for not conforming to society's constrictive rules and regulations. As Alain Silver and James Ursini write in *The Gangster Film Reader*, these "Hollywood anti-heroes took action, tried to beat the system [and] did something with their lot in life."

The pirate image is similar. As historian Colin Woodard wrote about real-life Golden Age pirates, "So great were these pirates' reputations—daring antiheroes, noble brigands—that they've been sustained ever since, inspiring 18th-century plays, 19th-century novels, and 20th- and 21st-century motion pictures, television shows and pop culture iconography." Author David Cordingly stresses that "pirates have acquired a romantic aura which they never had in the seventeenth century and which they certainly never deserved." Whether deserved or not, this aura has remained. In fact, Johnny Depp has said that he modeled Captain Jack Sparrow after Rolling Stones guitarist Keith Richards, whom Depp calls "the coolest rock and roll star of all time." (Richards played Jack Sparrow's father in 2007's *Pirates of the Caribbean: At World's End*.) As Depp told the website IGN, "I sort of thought that pirates would be the rock and roll stars of the 18th century, you know?"

SOURCE NOTES

9   Daniel Defoe, *A General History of the Pyrates* (Mineola, NY: Dover, 1999), 588.

14 Anders Winroth, *The Age of the Vikings* (Princeton, NJ: Princeton University Press, 2014), 20.

20 "Captain Kidd," Mudcat Café, accessed March 24, 2015, http://mudcat.org /@displaysong.cfm?SongID=1085.

21 Ibid.

24 David Cordingly, *Under the Black Flag: The Romance and Reality of Life among the Pirates* (New York: Random House, 1995), 113–114.

25 David Rickman and Angus Konstam, *Pirate: The Golden Age* (Newbury, UK: Osprey, 2011), 32.

29 Henry Louis Gates Jr., "Were There Black Pirates?," *Root*, July 28, 2014, http://www .theroot.com/articles/history/2014/07/black_pirates_were_there_any.html.

31 Katy Winter, "Beating Your Wife Is Fine . . . if You're a Baron—and Other Rules from 17th Century Book of Women's Rights, up for Auction at £3,000," *Daily Mail* (London), January 22, 2014, http://www.dailymail.co.uk/femail/article-2543890/First-English -book-womens-rights-17th-century-sell-3-000.html.

33 Cordingly, *Under the Black Flag*, 64.

34 Defoe, *General History*, 152.

35 Ibid., 194–196.

48 Anita Gates, "The Happy Return of the Pirate King and His Loyal Swashbucklers," *New York Times*, November 26, 2006, http://www.nytimes.com/2006/11/26/nyregion /nyregionspecial2/26cttheater.html?_r=0.

58 Ann Hornaday, "'Captain Phillips' Movie Review: Tom Hanks's Superb Performance Anchors Thrilling Tale," *Washington Post*, October 10, 2013, http://www.washingtonpost .com/goingoutguide/movies/captain-phillips-movie-review-tom-hankss-superb -performance-anchors-thrilling-tale/2013/10/09/f2fab7ea-2f65-11e3-bbed -a8a60c601153_story.html.

62 Alain Silver and James Ursini, eds., *Gangster Film Reader* (New York: Limelight Editions, 2007), 260.

62 Colin Woodard, "The Last Days of Blackbeard," *Smithsonian*, February 2014, http:// www.smithsonianmag.com/history/last-days-blackbeard-180949440/?all&no-ist.

63 Cordingly, *Under the Black Flag*, xiv.

63 Michelle Zoromski, "A Conversation with Johnny Depp," IGN, July 11, 2003, http://www.ign.com/articles/2003/07/11/a-conversation-with-johnny-depp.

GLOSSARY

antihero: a main character in a movie, a book, or another story who lacks typical or conventional heroic qualities

boatswain: a ship's officer tasked with taking care of equipment

buccaneers: French, British, and Dutch sea adventurers who preyed on Spanish settlements and ships in the Americas in the seventeenth century. Buccaneers looted, raided, and pillaged just like pirates. Like privateers, they attacked the ships of political and commercial rivals of their native countries. Also like privateers, they often had letters of marque from the governments they served.

corsairs: pirates hired by various nations to attack enemy vessels on the Mediterranean Sea. Corsairs were similar to buccaneers and privateers.

galleons: square-rigged sailing vessels used from the sixteenth century to the early eighteenth century, either as warships or cargo ships. Galleons were commonly used by Spanish sailors.

grappling hook: a multipronged hook attached to a rope. Pirates would use grappling hooks to snag an enemy vessel and would pull on the ropes to bring the pirate ship and the enemy ship together.

letters of marque: documents issued by European governments that authorized privateers to attack merchant ships of enemy nations

mutiny: a rebellion against authority, usually carried out by sailors or soldiers against their superior officers

pardon: the excusing of a crime or an offense, with no penalty given

pirate: someone who commits robbery on a body of water

privateer: a ship or a captain with a government-issued license to raid or attack enemy harbors or ships during wartime

protection racket: a scheme wherein a group of criminals demands payment from businesses. Those who don't pay are preyed upon by the criminals.

ransom: payment demanded for a prisoner's release

Royal Navy: the navy of the British Empire

tanker: a road vehicle, a ship, or an aircraft used specifically for carrying liquids, especially petroleum, in bulk

tribute: a payment made on a periodic basis by one nation or ruler to another, often in exchange for protection or some other service. From the seventeenth century to the nineteenth century, some European nations paid tribute to the Barbary States to keep themselves free of pirate attacks.

vigilantes: citizens who take the law into their own hands, without the legal authority to do so

SELECTED BIBLIOGRAPHY

Anthony, Robert J. *Pirates in the Age of Sail*. New York: W. W. Norton, 2007.

Barrie, J. M. *Peter Pan and Other Plays*. Oxford: Oxford University Press, 1995.

Bie, Michael. "The Life and Crimes of Dan Seavey." ClassicWisconsin.com. Accessed February 13, 2015. http://www.classicwisconsin.com/features/ourpirate.htm.

Boyd, Richard J. "Roaring Dan Seavey: The Pirate of Lake Michigan." *Michigan History*, May/June 2012. http://www.hsmichigan.org/wp-content/uploads/2012/04/DanSeavey.pdf.

Carrell, Toni L., "The U.S. Navy and the Anti-Piracy Patrol in the Caribbean." *Ocean Explorer*. Accessed February 13, 2015. http://oceanexplorer.noaa.gov/explorations/08trouvadore/background/piracy/piracy.html.

Cohat, Yves. *The Vikings: Lords of the Seas*. New York: Harry N. Abrams, 1992.

"Dan Seavey: A Great Lakes Pirate." Door County Maritime Museum. Accessed February 13, 2015. http://www.dcmm.org/gills-rock-museum/dan-seavey-a-great-lakes-pirate/.

Dorsey, Joe. "25 Historical Facts about the Captain Phillips Somali Pirate Kidnapping." *Travel Thru History*. Accessed January 31, 2014. http://www.travelthruhistory.tv/25-historical-facts-captain-phillips-somali-pirate-kidnapping/.

Esposito, Richard, John Berman, and Aaron Katersky. "Pirate Suspect Sobs in Court: 'I Have No Money.'" *ABC News*, April 21, 2009. http://abcnews.go.com/Blotter/story?id=7386881.

Geringer, Joseph. "Jean Lafitte: Gentleman Pirate of New Orleans." *Crime Library*. Accessed February 13, 2015. http://www.crimelibrary.com/gangsters_outlaws/cops_others/lafitte/1.html.

Goldman, William. *The Princess Bride: S. Morganstern's Classic Tale of True Love and High Adventure*. New York: Ballantine, 1998.

Hefele, Matt, Mark Sarosky, Ryan Elkadi, and Andrew Jyegal. "Gnaeus Pompeius Magnus." Pennsylvania State University. Accessed February 13, 2015. http://sites.psu.edu/firsttriumvirate/pompey/.

Hogan, Michael D. "Pirates of the Carolinas (Part VI): Henry Avery, the Arch Pirate." *Southport NC and Greater Brunswick County*. Accessed February 13, 2015. http://www.southportncmagazine.com/pirates_vi.html.

Holland, Luke. "Black Sails: Real Men Don't Play Football, They Shoot Cannons." *Guardian* (London), June 25, 2014. http://www.theguardian.com/tv-and-radio/tvandradioblog/2014/jun/25/not-the-world-cup-black-sails-toby-stephens.

Kates, Kristi. "Pirates of the Great Lakes." *Northern Express*, September 16, 2013. http://www.northernexpress.com/michigan/article-6127-pirates-of-the-great-lakes.html.

Kirkpatrick, Jennifer. "Blackbeard: Pirate Terror at Sea." *NationalGeographic.com*. Accessed February 13, 2015. http://www.nationalgeographic.com/pirates/bbeard.html.

Moore, Michael Scott. "We Were Pirates Once, and Young: An American Way to Understand Somali Pirates." *New Republic*, October 22, 2011. http://www.newrepublic.com/article /world/96345/pirates-history-america-somalia-wealth.

Morris, Joseph. "The Origins of the Sea Peoples." Florida State University. Accessed February 13, 2015. http://web.archive.org/web/20060903164435/http://dscholarship.lib.fsu .edu/cgi/viewcontent.cgi?article=1199&context=undergrad.

Paskin, Willa. "Avast Wasteland." *Slate*, May 30, 2014. http://www.slate.com/articles/arts /television/2014/05/john_malkovich_pirate_drama_crossbones_reviewed.html.

Pennell, C. R., ed. *Bandits at Sea: A Pirates Reader*. New York: New York University Press, 2001.

Pinsker, Joe. "The Pirate Economy." *Atlantic*, May 2014, 88–89.

"Piracy: A Brief History of Piracy." Royal Naval Museum Library. Accessed February 13, 2015. http://www.royalnavalmuseum.org/info_sheets_piracy.htm.

"Pirates in the Atlantic World." Smithsonian National Museum of American History. Accessed February 13, 2015. http://amhistory.si.edu/onthewater/exhibition/1_5.html.

Rediker, Marcus. *Villains of All Nations: Atlantic Pirates in the Golden Age*. Boston: Beacon, 2004.

Roff, Peter. "Pirates on the High (Internet) Seas." *US News*, February 21, 2014. http://www .usnews.com/opinion/blogs/peter-roff/2014/02/21/ip-pirates-make-a-bundle-off-the -internet.

"Somali Pirates a Far Cry from Buccaneers of Old." *Washington Times*, April 11, 2009. http:// www.washingtontimes.com/news/2009/apr/11/somali-pirates-a-far-cry-from -buccaneers-of-old/?page=1.

Souza, Philip. "Ancient Rome and the Pirates." *History Today* 51, no. 7 (2001). http://www .historytoday.com/philip-souza/ancient-rome-and-pirates.

Stewart-Seume, Bryony. "Welcome Henry Every. 'You're a PIRATE!'" *AllThingsUncharted.com*, November 15, 2013. http://allthingsuncharted.com/2013/11/welcome-henry-every -youre-a-pirate/.

Woodard, Colin. "Anne Bonny." *The Republic of Pirates*. Accessed February 13, 2015. http:// www.republicofpirates.net/Bonny.html.

———. *The Republic of Pirates*. New York: Harcourt, 2007.

Yosomono, Eric, and Jean Flynn. "The 7 Most Terrifying Pirates from History." *Cracked*, August 19, 2011. http://www.cracked.com/article_19353_the-7-most-terrifying-pirates-from -history.html.

Yosomono, Eric, and Drew Miller. "6 Absurd Pirate Myths Everyone Believes (Thanks to Movies)." *Cracked*, October 21, 2011. http://www.cracked.com/article_19482_6 -absurd-pirate-myths-everyone-believes-thanks-to-movies.html.

FOR FURTHER INFORMATION

BOOKS

Fiction

Barrie, J. M. *Peter Pan: Peter and Wendy and Peter Pan in Kensington Gardens.* New York: Penguin Classics, 2004.

David, Peter. *Tigerheart.* New York: Ballantine, 2008.

Meyer, L. A. *Bloody Jack: Being an Account of the Curious Adventures of Mary "Jacky" Faber, Ship's Boy.* New York: HMH Books for Young Readers, 2010.

Stevenson, Robert Louis. *Treasure Island.* Minneapolis: First Avenue Editions, 2015.

Nonfiction

Cordingly, David. *Under the Black Flag: The Romance and the Reality of Life among the Pirates.* New York: Random House, 1996.

Defoe, Daniel. *A General History of the Pyrates.* Minneola, NY: Dover, 1999.

Donaldson, Madeline. *Pirates, Scoundrels, and Scallywags.* Minneapolis: Lerner Publications, 2013.

January, Brendan. *The Aftermath of the Wars against the Barbary Pirates.* Minneapolis: Twenty-First Century Books, 2009.

Kritzler, Edward. *Jewish Pirates of the Caribbean.* New York: Doubleday, 2008.

Phillips, Richard. *A Captain's Duty: Somali Pirates, Navy SEALS, and Dangerous Days at Sea.* New York: Hachette, 2011.

Sjoholm, Barbara. *The Pirate Queen: In Search of Grace O'Malley and Other Legendary Women of the Sea.* Berkeley, CA: Seal, 2004.

Woodard, Colin. *The Republic of Pirates: Being the True and Surprising Story of the Caribbean Pirates and the Man Who Brought Them Down.* New York: Mariner, 2008.

WEBSITES

Mariners' Museum and Park
http://www.marinersmuseum.org
This site from the Mariners' Museum in Newport News, Virginia, includes information on pirates, as well as other aspects of sailing and seafaring.

Royal Naval Museum Library
http://www.royalnavalmuseum.org
The website of the Royal Naval Museum of the United Kingdom includes information on pirates as well as sailors of the British Royal Navy.

Voyage to Discovery
http://www.voyagetodiscovery.org
This website is devoted to the stories of Africans at sea, including those who crossed the oceans as slaves, those who became pirates, and those who commanded ships.

FILMS

True Caribbean Pirates. DVD. New York: History Channel, 2006.
This documentary film explore pirates of the Golden Age, including Anne Bonny, Bartholomew Roberts, and Blackbeard.

Vikings. DVD. London: British Broadcasting Corporation, 2012.
This documentary from the British Broadcasting Corporation explores Viking culture as well as the exploits of Viking raiders.

INDEX

PHOTO ACKNOWLEDGMENTS

The images in this book are used with the permission of: © iStockphoto.com/Ivan Bajic (old paper) © iStockphoto.com/Gordan1 (grunge frame); © Patrick Eden/Alamy, p. 1; © iStockphoto.com/Ivan Bliznetsov, p. 3; Walt Disney Pictures/Newscom, p. 4; © Captain Avery capturing the 'Ganj-i-Sawai' on 8th September 1695 (engraving), English School, (18th century)/Private Collection/Bridgeman Images, p. 7; © Joyner Library/East Carolina University, p. 8; © Laura Westlund/Independent Picture Service, pp. 12–13; © Costa/Leemage/Bridgeman Images, p. 14; © Leemage/UIG/Getty Images, p. 16; © RDImages/Epics/Hulton Fine Art Collection/Getty Images, p. 19; © Pictorial Press Ltd/Alamy, pp. 22, 32; © Universal History Archive/Getty Images, p. 27; The Granger Collection, New York, p. 30; © Leemage/Universal Images Group/Getty Images, p. 35; Naval Historical Center, Department of the Navy, Washington Navy Yard/Wikimedia Commons (public domain), p. 39; © Lebrecht Music and Arts Photo Library/Alamy, pp. 40, 49; U.S. Coast Guard, p. 43; © Images & Stories/Alamy, p. 45; Walt Disney/Kobal Collection/Art Resource, NY, p. 52; © John Springer Collection/CORBIS, p. 54; © Moviestore collection Ltd/Alamy, p. 56; © Doug Benc/Getty Images, p. 61; © Candela Foto Art/Kreuziger/Getty Images, p. 63; Michael De Luca Productions/Kobal Collection/Art Resource, NY, p. 69.

Front cover: © FlamingPumpkin/E+/Getty Images (swords); © iStockphoto.com/vectomart (flames); © iStockphoto.com/NREY (skull with eye patch). Back cover: © iStockphoto.com/Evgeny Sergeev.

ABOUT THE AUTHOR

Arie Kaplan is an award-winning nonfiction author and screenwriter. He has written comic book stories and graphic novels for DC Comics, Archie Comics, Bongo Comics, Penguin Young Readers Group, and other publishers. He is the author of many books for young adult readers, including *Saturday Night Live: Shaping TV Comedy and American Culture* (2014) and *American Pop: Hit Makers, Superstars, and Dance Revolutionaries* (2012). His book *From Krakow to Krypton: Jews and Comic Books* was a finalist for the 2008 National Jewish Book Award. Kaplan has also written jokes and comedy sketches for the television series *TruTV Presents: World's Dumbest* and humor articles for *MAD* magazine. He is married to a beautiful, brilliant Jamaican woman who—as far as she knows—is not the descendant of Caribbean pirates. Check out his website at www.ariekaplan.com.